IMAGES

Games

Karen Bryant-Mole

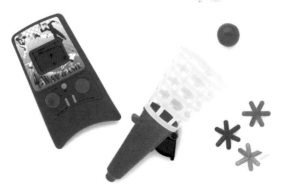

Heinemann

First published in Great Britain by Heinemann Library, Halley Court, Jordan Hill, Oxford OX2 8EJ,
a division of Reed Educational & Professional Publishing Ltd.

OXFORD FLORENCE PRAGUE MADRID ATHENS MELBOURNE AUCKLAND KUALA LUMPUR
SINGAPORE TOKYO IBADAN NAIROBI KAMPALA JOHANNESBURG GABORONE
PORTSMOUTH NH (USA) CHICAGO MEXICO CITY SAO PAULO

Designed by Jean Wheeler
Commissioned photography by Zul Mukhida
Produced by Mandarin Offset Ltd.
Printed and bound in China

01 00 99 98 97
10 9 8 7 6 5 4 3 2 1

ISBN 0 431 06309 5

British Library Cataloguing in Publication Data
Bryant-Mole, Karen
Games. - (Images)
1.Games - Juvenile literature 2.Readers (Primary)
I.Title
688.7

**Some of the more difficult words in this book are
explained in the glossary.**

Acknowledgements
The Publishers would like to thank the following for permission to reproduce photographs. Chapel Studios; 8 (right)
Zul Mukhida, Tony Stone Images; 9 (top) Jo Browne/Mick Smee, 9 (bottom) Lori Adamski Peek, 16 (left), 16 (right)
Dan Smith, 17 (left) Bob Thomas, 17 (right) Amwell, Zefa; 8 (left and back cover).

Every effort has been made to contact copyright holders of any material reproduced in this book. Any omissions will be
rectified in subsequent printings if notice is given to the Publisher.

Contents

Traditional

Traditional games have been played in the same way for many years.

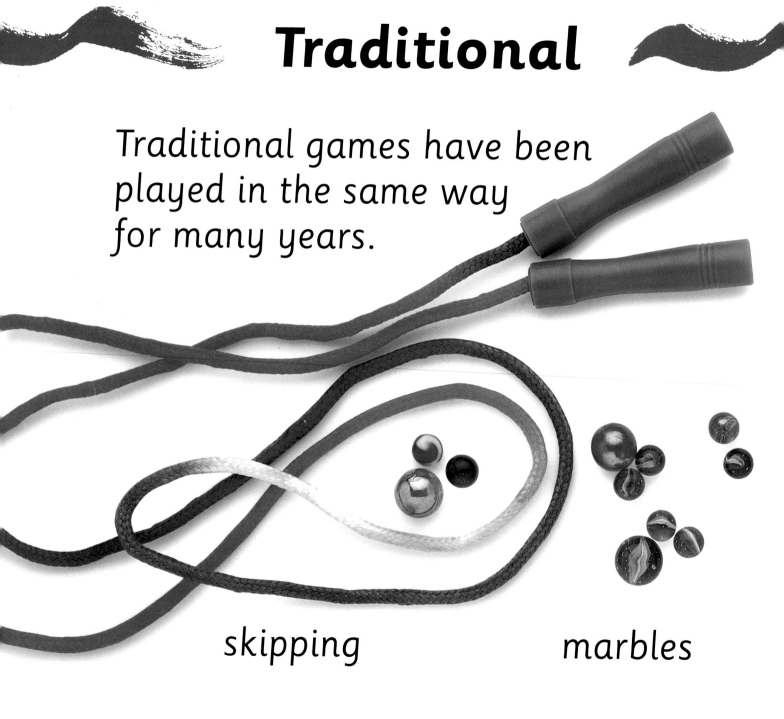

skipping

marbles

dominoes

noughts and crosses

Board games

Here are some games
that are played on
boards.

Do you have any board games at home or at school?

7

Outdoor games

Which of these games do
you like to play?

blind man's buff

clapping games

I spy

chase

9

Party games

Do you know how to play these party games?

pass the parcel

treasure hunt

musical chairs

Card games

There are lots of different card games.

happy families

picture
lotto

snap

pairs

What is your favourite card game?

Ball games

Some games have to be played with a special type of ball.

soccer ball

tennis balls

basketball

American
football

golf balls

Team games

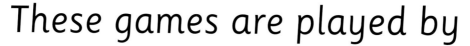

These games are played by two groups of people, or teams.

baseball

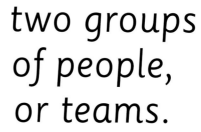

rugby

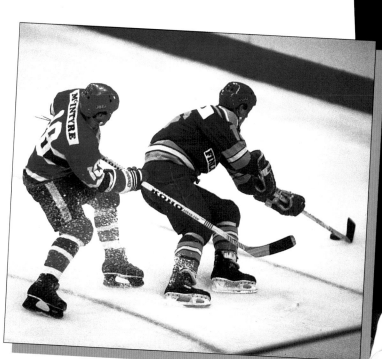

ice hockey

lacrosse

You can play
these games
by yourself.

Learning games

Learning is fun with these games.

matching
pictures

learning
numbers

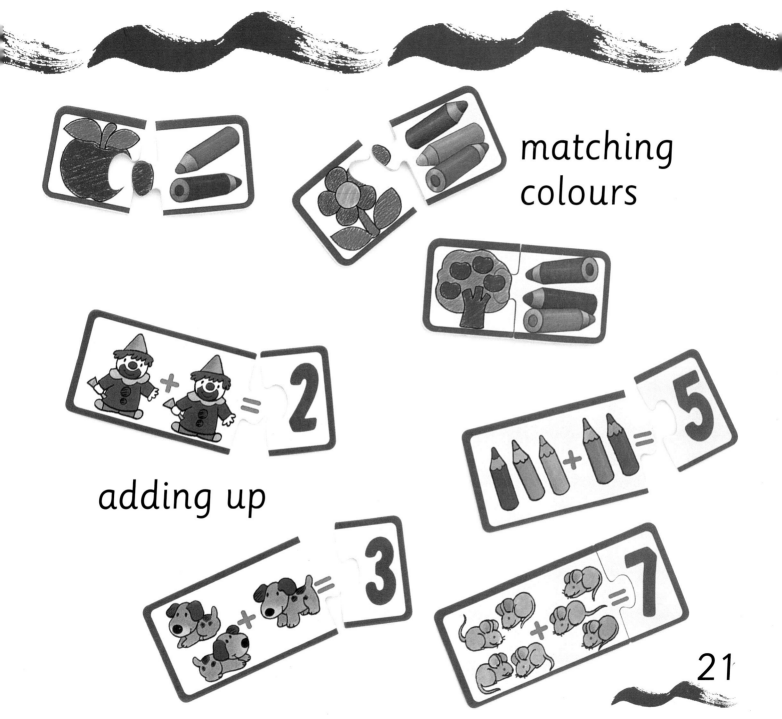

matching colours

adding up

21

Travel games

Travel games are usually smaller than ordinary games.

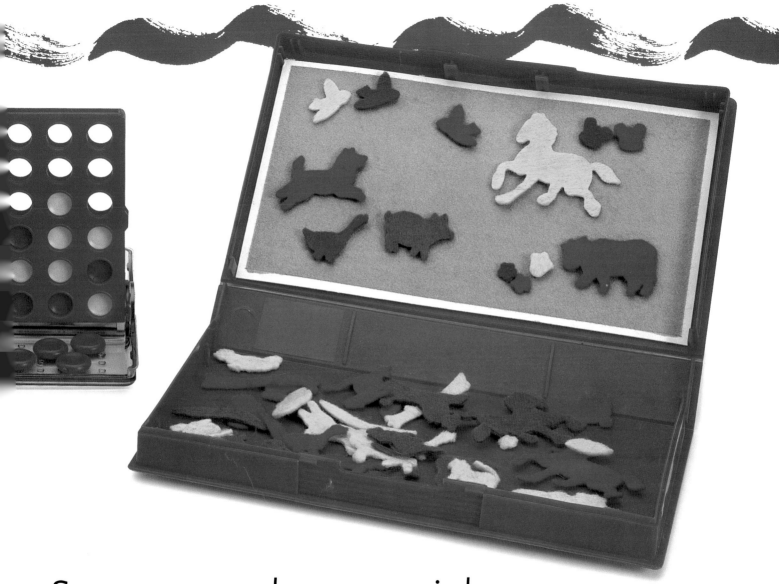

Some games have special
playing pieces that will not slip off.

Glossary

musical chairs a game in which you have to find a chair to sit on when the music playing on the tape recorder stops

pass the parcel a game in which you have to unwrap layers of paper from a parcel to get to a prize

snap a game for two players in which you try to win cards by being the first to spot that two cards are the same

Index